Jumb

written by Kaye

illustrated by Tom Clayton

THE CAST

BEN    **SAM**    **JOJO**    **MOUSE**

MUM
(Trish Macdonald)

DAD
(Martin Macdonald)

Scene 1

The twin's bedroom. It is morning. Jojo jumps out of bed. Mouse is asleep.

JOJO   Mouse! Wake up. It's Saturday!

MOUSE   What?

JOJO   It's Saturday morning. Up you get.

She tries to pull off the quilt. Mouse holds on.

MOUSE   Stop it. I'm tired. Leave me alone, Jojo.

JOJO   Come on. The sun's out. Ben and Sam will be here soon.

MOUSE   I want to stay in bed. Go away!

Scene 2

The kitchen. Dad is making breakfast. Mum is feeding Pip.

Enter Jojo.

DAD Hello, Jojo. Where is Mouse?

JOJO He's cross. He won't get up.

She sits and eats her cereal.

DAD That's not like Mouse.

MUM I hope he's not sick. I'll go up and see him.

Exit Mum.

The doorbell rings.

JOJO That's Ben and Sam. I'm off!

DAD Have a nice time.

Exit Jojo.

Scene 3

Ben and Sam wait outside the house. Jojo opens the door.

BEN   Hello, Jojo.

SAM   Where is Mouse?

JOJO   In bed. He won't get up.

BEN   That's funny.

SAM   Has he got chicken pox?

JOJO   I don't think so.

BEN   So why won't he get up?

JOJO   Who cares? He's grumpy today. Come on. Let's go and play.

All exit to the park.

Scene 4

The kitchen. Dad is clearing up.

Enter Mouse.

DAD   Hello, Mouse. Do you want breakfast?

MOUSE   No thanks. I'm not hungry.

DAD   Where are you going?

MOUSE   Just out.

Exit Mouse.

Enter Mum.

MUM   Where is he?

DAD   He's gone out.

MUM   Oh dear.

DAD   Is he sick, do you think?

MUM   Not sick. Just sad. Look what I found under his pillow.

She has a photo of Lucky, the rabbit.

DAD Poor old Mouse. He misses Lucky a lot.

Enter Jojo.

JOJO Hello. I forgot my skipping rope.

MUM Have you seen Mouse, Jojo?

JOJO No. Is he up, then?

MUM Yes. He's gone out. Will you go and look for him, please?

JOJO Why? He's so grumpy today.

DAD He's not really cross. He's missing Lucky.

JOJO I miss him too. He was my rabbit as well.

MUM Yes. But Mouse always cleaned out Lucky's hutch on Saturdays.

DAD This is the first Saturday without him.

JOJO Oh, I see. Poor Mouse.

MUM Will you see if you can find him?

DAD We don't want him to be on his own, feeling sad.

JOJO I'll find him. I think I know where he is.

MUM Thank you, Jojo.

Exit Jojo.

Scene 5

The secret room. Mouse sits all alone. He is sad.

Enter Jojo, Ben and Sam.

JOJO Mouse? Can we come in?

MOUSE Go away.

BEN We don't have to talk if you don't want to.

SAM We can just sit here quietly.

MOUSE Look, I'm fine. Why don't you just go and play?

BEN It's not so much fun without you.

SAM We miss you.

JOJO   I know you feel sad about Lucky. I do too.

MOUSE   He was such a great rabbit.

SAM   He was. I always wished he was mine.

BEN   I would feel the same if I lost Fatcat.

MOUSE   I always cleaned his hutch out on Saturday mornings.

SAM   I used to come and help sometimes. I liked doing that.

MOUSE   I wish he was still here.

JOJO Me too.

MOUSE I'm sorry I was grumpy, Jojo.

JOJO You were sad, that's all.

MOUSE Yes. Lucky was my friend.

BEN But you still have us.

MOUSE That's true. Thank you for being so nice. I feel better now.

BEN Do you want to come and play? It's sunny outside.

MOUSE All right.

SAM Race you to the pond!

All exit, running.

Scene 6

The twin's kitchen. Mum, Dad and Pip stand around the table. On the table is something big and square, covered with a cloth.

Enter Jojo and Mouse. Mouse looks more cheerful.

MUM Hello, you two. Ready for lunch?

MOUSE Yes, please. I'm starving.

JOJO What is that?

DAD A little surprise. Do you want to take the cloth off, Mouse?

Slowly, Mouse takes off the cloth. It is a cage. Inside is a tiny hamster.

JOJO A hamster! Oh, Dad! For us?

DAD Yes.

JOJO	Hooray! I have always wanted a hamster. Oh, he's so sweet.
MUM	What do you think, Mouse?
	Everyone looks at Mouse. Mouse says nothing.
DAD	He was the only hamster left in the pet shop.
MUM	Dad said he looked rather sad.
MOUSE	Did he? It's horrible, being sad.
DAD	I think he needs someone to love him. Like Lucky had.
JOJO	We will, won't we, Mouse?
MOUSE	Yes. We will.

JOJO   Can I take him out?

MUM   Let him get used to us. He will be shy at first.

JOJO   He's so small.

DAD   What shall we call him?

JOJO   Mouse can choose.

MOUSE   I know. Let's call him – Jumbo!

Everyone laughs at Mouse's funny idea. Mouse joins in.

THE END